T0193118

CALLED TO
BE ME

PASTOR CEE

WESTBOW
PRESS®
A DIVISION OF THOMAS NELSON
& ZONDERVAN

Copyright © 2021 Pastor Cee.

All rights reserved. No part of this book may be used or reproduced by any means, graphic, electronic, or mechanical, including photocopying, recording, taping or by any information storage retrieval system without the written permission of the author except in the case of brief quotations embodied in critical articles and reviews.

WestBow Press books may be ordered through booksellers or by contacting:

WestBow Press
A Division of Thomas Nelson & Zondervan
1663 Liberty Drive
Bloomington, IN 47403
www.westbowpress.com
844-714-3454

Because of the dynamic nature of the Internet, any web addresses or links contained in this book may have changed since publication and may no longer be valid. The views expressed in this work are solely those of the author and do not necessarily reflect the views of the publisher, and the publisher hereby disclaims any responsibility for them.

Any people depicted in stock imagery provided by Getty Images are models, and such images are being used for illustrative purposes only.
Certain stock imagery © Getty Images.

Scripture marked (KJV) taken from the King James Version of the Bible. Scripture quotations marked (AMPCE) are taken from the Amplified Bible, Copyright © 1954, 1958, 1962, 1964, 1965, 1987 by The Lockman Foundation. Used by permission.

Scripture quotations marked (NLT) are taken from the Holy Bible, New Living Translation, copyright ©1996, 2004, 2015 by Tyndale House Foundation. Used by permission of Tyndale House Publishers, a Division of Tyndale House Ministries, Carol Stream, Illinois 60188. All rights reserved.

ISBN: 978-1-6642-3266-2 (sc)
ISBN: 978-1-6642-3267-9 (hc)
ISBN: 978-1-6642-3265-5 (e)

Library of Congress Control Number: 2021908493

Print information available on the last page.

WestBow Press rev. date: 07/24/2021

I dedicate this work to all of those whom I have loved and lost. You all have touched my life in so many ways and I am forever grateful. Thank you for sharing your world with me and I will cherish the memories. Forever with me, Big Mama, Pinkey, Aunt Willie C., Aunt Estelle, Aunt Roselle, Aunt Johnell, and my Aunt Frankie.

To my late mother, Pearl Washington, who loved me and walked me through my chastening seasons (Hebrews 12:6–7). Thank you, Mama, for always praying for me and for allowing me to find refuge on your couch when life got hard. I know that you are still riding with me. You are my strength, my intercessor, and my biggest cheerleader. I love you, Mama.

To my big little sister, Barbara Hawkins, I miss your love, laughter, and colorful stories. You dreamed it, and I wish you were here to see God do it. I love you always, Bo.

To my girl, Courtney Woods, who is no longer with me. I miss you and our daily conversations dearly. You saw me, yet you loved me beyond my flaws. You encouraged me, and you spoke to the greatness in me. You are my angel and my forever armor bearer. Love you, Cokie.

To my late bishop, Bishop B. B. Willis Sr., who taught me so much about God, people, and life. You believed in me before I knew me, and you were always nudging me toward my destiny. I will cherish every moment we shared, and I will carry this mantle with respect, humility, and integrity to honor your legacy and your memory. Love you, Paw Paw.

CONTENTS

ACKNOWLEDGMENTS

This project was one of the greatest undertakings I have attempted. The journey was challenging, but God placed people in the right places at the right time, and they were essential to the conception and manifestation of this venture.

To my husband, Jacques, and our children, Jackie, Desmond, Xavier, and C'Aira, thank you for investing in me. Thank you for encouraging me and seeing me beyond where I am today. Each of you have been vital in propelling me toward the greatness God has for me. You all are the best. Your continuous love and support strengthened me on this journey, and I couldn't have done it without you. I love you all forever.

To Hillary Jackson, my "personal" editor, we did it! Thank you for the countless hours you spent reading and analyzing every word, sentence, scripture, and paragraph. I knew you were the right person. You were mean with that red pen, but because of it, I believe many people will be blessed.

To the women of BVW Fellowship, this was birthed out of the times you entrusted me to walk with you as you journeyed to your place of self-discovery. Thank you for your never-ending love and support of what God has purposed through me and for me. This is only the beginning.

To the Word Church family. Thank you for believing in me. We ride together! We rise together! Word Church for life!

INTRODUCTION

Your occupation may not be the same as others, but your purpose is similar. You were purposed to an occupation in life that would bring glory to the Father. Before walking into your vocation, complete your first assignment, which is being you:

> Before I formed thee in the belly I knew thee; and before thou camest forth out of the womb I sanctified thee, and I ordained thee. (Jeremiah 1:5 KJV)

These were God's words to Jeremiah at a time when Jeremiah was feeling inadequate and insignificant. Jeremiah was rejecting his call to action because he felt he was too young and deficient in speech:

> Then said I, "Ah, Lord God! behold, I cannot speak: for I am a child." (Jeremiah 1:6 KJV)

Jeremiah's flaw was not that he couldn't accomplish the task because he had not attempted the job. His flaw was his inability to see himself beyond his deficiencies. God knew what He had created Jeremiah to be and what was placed within him. Therefore, God looked beyond what Jeremiah considered to be a defect and spoke to his purpose, his "being."

God is seeking a people who will be themselves and allow Him to use their God-given personalities, gifts, skills, and talents to bless generations. God responds to Jeremiah by reprimanding him:

> Say not, I am a child: for thou shalt go to all that I shall send thee, and whatsoever I command thee thou shalt speak. (Jeremiah 1:7 KJV)

In other words, I've got you. Don't sell yourself short by limiting who you are to what you can do. God is speaking the same thing to you:

I have strength for all things in Christ Who empowers me [I am ready for anything and equal to anything through Him Who infuses inner strength into me; I am self-sufficient in Christ's sufficiency]." (Philippians 4:13 AMPC)

You may think you lack the skills to complete the task. You are wrong. You are capable of accomplishing your assignment because you have everything you need. You can do what you were created to do when you know yourself. The power is not in your skills, your gifts, or your talents. The power is in knowing yourself. Skills you learn, talents you develop, and gifts you use to achieve your purpose, so don't rely on them, but use them to express who you are: your essence, your passions, and your personality.

Just be you. Being you is accepting your personality and embracing the qualities that make you unique and different. You are self-sufficient. How many times have you passed over opportunities because you felt deficient? How many times have you failed to seize the moment because you felt unimportant?

God's got the ability. He just needs you to embrace yourself and realize that it is in Him that you live, move, and have your being. It is through Him that you are able to live your life beyond your limitations. Your limitations are self-imposed excuses that keep you from reaching beyond where you are or what you are doing. You must allow Him to break the limitations so you can be all that He created within you to be. He is requesting, demanding, and giving an order for you to be brought into action!

Called to Be ME is a work inspired by the Holy Spirit that will cause you to rise and become the you the Creator fashioned you to be. I spent many years searching for fulfillment and significance. I was looking for me through my accomplishments and through the applause of others, but I needed to see me, love me, and embrace me. The silent moments, accolades, and achievements did not define me; only God can define me.

God knew me before I was conceived, and before I was born, God designed me and called me when no one recognized me. When I found myself in Him, it became easier for me to identify my design and realize my purpose. The same can be true for you. You will not be fulfilled in life until you are being who you were created to be. Find you, and you will find your purpose, your passion, and your power for life.

This is your time for exploration. It is time for you to go on an expedition and discover yourself. The greatest and most valuable treasure is getting ready to be unraveled. That treasure is you.

Called to Be ME

But whatever I am now, it is all because God poured out
His special favor on me—and not without results.
—1 Corinthians 15:10 (NLT)

If you look up the word *call* in the dictionary, you will find several definitions. Sometimes your definition of a word is not as broad as the actual definition of that word; therefore, you are limited in knowledge and usage. This limits your ability to use and function within the scope of all that the word means. *Merriam-Webster* has several meanings for the word *call*, but a few of them stood out to me, and I want to share them with you.

I have chosen to use the following definitions, and I believe they will be important in the unfolding of the revelation that God wants to share in this work:

- to make a request or demand to come or be present
- to give order for; bring into action
- to summon to a particular activity, employment, or office[1]

All of us are called to do certain work. Some are apostles. Some are prophets, pastors, teachers, or evangelists. Some are called to the ministries of healing (doctor, nurse, surgeon, psychologist), helping (lawyer, secretary, accountant, schoolteacher, caterer), administration (company chairman, superintendent, principal), or government (president, mayor, legislator, governor).

Your vocation may be different than others, but you were created to bring glory to the Father, which makes you similar to everyone. How do you bring glory to the Father? Being you brings Him glory. Before you get to the work, fulfill your first call, which is you. God is making a demand for a people who will allow Him to use their gifts, skills, and talents. He is calling for the you He created. Stop trying to be like other people. You

[1] *Merriam-Webster*, s.v. "call (*v.*)," accessed July 17, 2020, http://www.merriam-webster.com/dictionary/call.

were uniquely designed for a reason. God created you, and He wants to work in you, through you, for you, and upon you:

> Wherefore, my beloved, as ye have always obeyed, not as
> in my presence only, but now much more in my absence,
> work out your own salvation with fear and trembling. For
> it is God which worketh in you both to will and to do of
> his good pleasure. (Philippians 2:12–13 KJV)

The work begins in you to bring freedom to you in order to be effective when it flows through you. You will achieve your freedom within you by using the Word to resolve any inner struggles in your mind, your will, or your emotions.

God believes in you, and He believes that you are worth the effort of His time and resources.

> God is all the while effectually at work in you [energizing
> and creating in you the power and desire] both to will and
> to work for His good pleasure and satisfaction and delight.
> (Philippians 2:13 AMPC)

You need to have that same belief about yourself. When did you stop believing in yourself? Where did you lose yourself? He is waiting on you to discover yourself and be yourself. He called you and purposed you from your mother's womb. Everything about you He designed, and He destined you according to His purpose. Your eyes, complexion, hair color, size, personality, gifts, and talents are a part of His desired makeup for your life. You have to believe that God made no mistakes when He created you. Accept, love, and appreciate the person you are. Just be yourself!

Affirmation

- I love and accept myself completely as I am.
- I don't have to try to please anyone else.
- I like myself, and that's what counts.
- I am highly pleasing to myself in the presence of other people.

- I express myself freely, fully, and easily.
- I am a powerful, loving, and creative being.
- I enjoy being me!

Say the affirmation above. Make it a part of your daily meditation. Now write your own affirmation that describes what you believe about yourself.

_____

_____

_____

_____

_____

_____

_____

_____

_____

_____

_____

_____

_____

_____

_____

_____

Self-Identity

*I have strength for all things in Christ Who empowers me [I am
ready for anything and equal to anything through Him Who infuses
inner strength into me; I am self-sufficient in Christ's sufficiency].*
—Philippians 4:13 (AMPC)

How do you see yourself? To live a purposeful and fulfilled life, you must
have a strong self-identity. An identity is the distinguishing character that
sets you apart from those around you. It is what makes you you. Do you
know what inherent quality of your character sets you apart from others?
Do you know what makes you unique? If you do not know, then it's time
to discover yourself. You are worth knowing! Discovering who you are
identifies who you're not. You are a customized model who God took His
time to fashion. No one has your style, flavor, or flair. Take the time to
study yourself, develop a strong self-identity, and identify your place in
this world.

One reason you need a strong self-identity is that you have to see
it to achieve it. A distorted self-image will cause you to turn from your
purpose. You must have self-value and be satisfied with your gifts, talents,
and abilities. If not, you turn from who you are, disabling (to cripple and
deprive of strength[2]) the power of God in your life.

Numbers 13 gives the account of the twelve spies who were sent
into Canaan to spy out the land. In verses 25–33, the spies return with
conflicting reports. They all agreed that the land was a prosperous land
that "floweth with milk and honey" (Numbers 13:27 KJV). They even
brought back the fruit as proof of the wealth of the land. They all agreed
that the people who dwelled in the land were strong and that the "cities
are walled, and very great" (Numbers 13:28 KJV).

They agreed that their enemies—the Amalekites, Hittites, Jebusites,
Amorites, and the children of Anak—had possession of the land. The
conflict in their report was with how they saw themselves. Two of them

---

[2] *Merriam-Webster*, s.v. "disabling (*v.*)," accessed July 17, 2020, http://www.merriam-webster.com/dictionary/disabling.

wanted to go get their stuff. They thought they were capable of overcoming the giants and walled cities.

On the other hand, the other ten said, "We be not able to go up against the people for they are stronger than we" (Numbers 13:31 KJV). They had a poor self-image, which hindered their ability to operate in power and authority. It kept them from moving forward and fulfilling their destinies. It was not their gifts, talents, or lack of skill. It was the perception they had of themselves that hindered their progress. The same can happen to you if how you see yourself conflicts with what God has prepared for you. God is a great God, and He has a great future in mind for you. There is greatness in you that you must see if you are going to achieve your purpose.

When God makes you a promise, He knows that you have everything within you to obtain what He has spoken. You are capable. He is not asking you to do it alone. You are self-sufficient, equal to all things, and able to do all things in Him. He just needs you to see the you He created, and He will do it through you. See yourself as capable. See yourself as strong. See yourself as smart. See yourself as intelligent. See yourself as powerful. See yourself as overcoming. See yourself living a fulfilled life. See it.

> And they brought up an evil report of the land which they had searched unto the children of Israel, saying, "The land, through which we have gone to search it, is a land that eateth up the inhabitants thereof and all the people that we saw in it are men of a great stature. And there we saw the giants, the sons of Anak, which come of the giants: and we were in our own sight as grasshoppers, and so we were in their sight." (Numbers 13:32–33 KJV)

Another reason you need a strong self-identity is because people see you as you see yourself. How do you present yourself to the people around you? Do they see a confident person who is excited about life's possibilities and about what lies ahead? Or do they see a struggling, unsure, and fearful individual?

People know when you have a swagger about yourself. That swagger is more intimidating than anything you can do or say. Years ago, I traveled with our church choir to sing at many musicals and gospel concerts. At times, we would see a group that would enter the building with a look that made us think, *Wow! They look like they could set the place on fire.* They had a demeanor about them that said, "We've got it going on." You have to be the same way about who you are and what you are capable of accomplishing.

When people see you, something about your appearance should exude self-confidence and self-respect. People should see you and believe in you. If you do not believe in yourself, who will? You cannot expect people to accept you when you do not accept yourself. In Numbers 13, the spies saw themselves as grasshoppers. Therefore, they believed the enemy had the same opinion. They were already defeated, and no battle was fought. If you see yourself as a winner, others will see you as a winner—and you will win!

Seven Elements of a Strong Self-Identity

The greatest way to destroy anything is to use it in error or outside of its purpose. Anything you don't value; you abuse and misuse. *Abuse* is defined as "to put to a wrong or improper use."[3]

When you don't recognize yourself, you operate outside of your intended design, which is abuse. In *Pursuit of Purpose*, Dr. Myles Munroe said, "Where purpose is not known, abuse is inevitable." To stop the self-abuse, develop and protect your self-identity because maintaining a sense of self-worth will release into your life confidence and power, giving you the strength to rise and fulfill your destiny. You should work on developing these seven elements and making them a part of your being to assist in maintaining your self-identity:

- deem valuable: to have value, confidence, and satisfaction in yourself; self-worth
- desire: an appetite to live your life
- dream: a creative imagination to envision all of your life's possibilities
- determinant: a reason for your existence; purpose

---

[3] *Merriam-Webster*, s.v. "abuse (*v.*)," accessed July 17, 2020, http://www.merriam-webster.com/dictionary/abuse.

- divine inspiration: an influencing, moving, guiding vision from God
- discipline: an ability to yield to purpose when it is not in agreement with current conditions
- determination: making a habit of remaining focused on your life's mission even in opposition; resolve

Three Enemies of Self-Identity

Even the devil knows the importance of a strong self-image. God gave Jesus His identity, and Jesus received what His Father said about Him. From the moment the voice came from heaven and declared, "This is my beloved Son, in whom I am well pleased" (Matthew 3:17 KJV) until He hung on the cross with the mocking inscription "This is Jesus, the King of the Jews" (Matthew 27:37 KJV), His self-image was always challenged by the enemy through the weapons of problems, people, and pain. The enemy is using the same weapons against you today. You must be able to identify the weapons the enemy is using against you in any season to destroy your self-image.

Problems: physical or environmental conditions that are difficult to deal with (Matthew 3:17–4:4)

Jesus fasted for forty days. When the fast was complete, He hungered, which is a physical problem. The devil challenged that problem by saying, "If thou be the Son of God" (Matthew 4:3 KJV). The devil heard God declare that Jesus was His Son. He knew who Jesus was, but the devil was hoping that he could use this problem to cast doubt.

The devil will take the opportunity to use problems to destroy your self-identity by causing you to identify your self-worth based on your ability to stand against a problem. The devil knows who you are. The enemy has made it his mission to keep that mystery hidden from you. He wants to keep the gift of your beautiful life concealed to keep you from walking in purpose and in fulfillment. The devil wants you to live your life in doubt, despair, depression, and doom because of a problem you are experiencing. Remember that trouble comes to *refine* you—not to *define* you. Do not let situations dictate who you are or what you can have because situations are temporary and subject to change.

People: their opinions and judgments (Luke 4:16–22)

When Jesus stood to declare His life's purpose and mission, they did not challenge His call, but they did challenge His identity: "And they said, 'Is not this Joseph's son?'" (Luke 4:22 KJV).

They wanted to minimize his ability to respond to the call by minimizing how He saw Himself to fit how they saw Him. They had problems with His identity. They could not equate His declaration of His call (preaching the gospel, healing, delivering, and giving sight to the blind) with the Jesus they grew up knowing.

People have already decided for you what they believe is an adequate way of being. They have made that decision based on your past failures, the failures or successes of your parents, or your current economic or educational status. At times, it will be difficult for people to see you and value you beyond those factors. *In Pursuit of Purpose,* Myles Munroe said, "Don't give others the right to say what kind of human value you have."

You must value yourself beyond the judgment of others. If people want to live in your past, let them. You keep moving forward. It's about you seeing yourself by maintaining God's image of you and continuing to strive to be all that He created you to be. When God created you, He did not consult people. You do not have to prove yourself to anyone but God. Even when God makes the change in your life for His glory, there will be skeptics who will be waiting on you to fail. They will not see what you see. It takes God to reveal purpose because purpose comes from Him.

God will not reveal His plan for your life to everybody. He will only reveal it to those He intended to walk with you during that season.

Jesus asked the disciples, "Whom do men say that I, the Son of man, am?" (Matthew 16:13 KJV). They replied, that some say you are Elias, others Jeremiah, or one of the prophets.

> Then He asked, "But whom say ye that I am? And Simon
> Peter answered and said, Thou art the Christ, the Son of
> the living God." (Matthew 16:15–16 KJV)

Jesus responded, "for flesh and blood hath not revealed it unto thee, but my Father which is in heaven" (Matthew 16:17 KJV).

God revealed it to Simon Peter because of purpose. After Jesus's ascension, Simon Peter stood and preached about the life, death, and resurrection of Jesus Christ with such conviction and revelation that thousands were saved.

No matter how spiritual people are, your purpose will be made known only to those who are destined to assist in maximizing your life's potential. It is crucial that you fellowship with people who know your purpose, support it, and have a desire to see you fulfill it. Surround yourself with individuals who are positive thinkers who are secure in their abilities, talents, and gifts. People who have a vision can see a vision for you. They will give you wisdom and motivate you toward what God reveals.

Pain: physical, emotional, or spiritual discomfort that causes suffering or distress (Mark 14:32–39)

According to Mark, the idea of the cross was beginning to take its toll upon Jesus. Mark states that He "began to be sore amazed, and to be very heavy; And saith unto them, 'My soul is exceeding sorrowful unto death'" (Mark 14:33–34 KJV).

The pain of the cross caused Jesus to question His ability to endure and fulfill His purpose. In a conversation with His Father, He says, "All things are possible unto Thee; take away this cup from Me" (Mark 14:36 KJV).

Things in life can cause so much pain that you begin to question your abilities and the possibility of fulfilling your destiny. You must realize that pain is a part of the process of fulfilling your life's purpose. The Word is inscribed with references, declarations, and testimonies to the reality that trouble, affliction, distress, and persecution are necessary to the backdrop of your life, and they play a part in your success. Opportunities ignite opposition:

> For a great door and effectual is opened unto me, and
> there are many adversaries. (1 Corinthians 16:9 KJV)

When you make the decision to begin to live your life according to purpose, the enemy will challenge you with painful situations. Do not stop! Pain may be necessary, but it is not the end of the journey. It often marks the birthing of a new and victorious you.

Pain has a purpose. You can overcome pain with an understanding of the purpose it has in your life. Jesus fulfilled purpose by way of the cross. According to Mark 8:31–32, He is expecting you to deny yourself, take up your cross, and follow Him. The cross represents a place of suffering, death, and a place where the flesh is crucified and brought into subjection to the will, desires, and purpose of God. On the cross, you will experience opposition, contradiction, obstruction, disruption, and betrayal. Be of good cheer! Because He overcame, so will you. You will overcome the pain of the cross. Your present suffering is "not worthy to be compared with the glory" (Romans 8:18 KJV) that will be revealed in you, through you, for you, and upon you. Keep moving. There is a glory waiting on you!

Two transitions occur in the process of suffering. One transition is the development of your character. Your response to pain will either mature you or maim you, which is to mutilate or damage.[4] Maturity takes place when you approach the pain by focusing on purpose. When you focus on purpose, you measure where you are compared to where you should be. You take a real look at the how and why, seeking to make any personal adjustments to weaknesses in character that are hindering your ability to overcome.

Maiming takes place when you approach the pain by focusing on the problem. In this case, your focus is the what and the who. What happened—and who made it happen? Seldom do you include yourself in this type of assessment. You tend to measure where you are with who is around you, making them responsible for your success or failure. Making them responsible means they will have to make the adjustments for you to be successful.

Other people will not take responsibility for your pain, which is hurtful, and it can damage your self-identity. Make it your aim to approach every challenge focused on the glory the Lord wants to reveal in you. As you continue to behold in the Word the glory of the Lord, you "are constantly being transfigured into His very own image in ever increasing splendor

---

[4] *Merriam-Webster*, s.v. "maim (*v.*)," accessed July 17, 2020, http://www.merriam-webster.com/dictionary/maim.

and from one degree of glory to another" (2 Corinthians 3:18 AMPC). There is a glory, which is the manifestation of God's Word in your life, that He reveals through suffering. Therefore, even in pain, stay focused on the glory that the Lord desires to reveal.

The other transition is the shifting from one state, stage, or place in life to another. God allows you to experience the fire and floods of life, but He does not leave you there. He promises to deliver you out of all of your afflictions:

> For thou, O God, hast proved us: thou hast tried us, as silver is tried. Thou broughtest us into the net; thou laidst affliction upon our loins. Thou hast caused men to ride over our heads; we went through fire and through water: but thou broughtest us out into a wealthy place. (Psalm 66:10–12 KJV)

He uses your wilderness experience as a place of transition with a plan to move you to your destiny and your place of abundance. Do not let people, pain, or problems cause you to be consumed and miss your promotion. See them for what they are—a challenge—and all challenges can be overcome. Don't yield your confidence to them. You might be tempted, but don't cast it away.

According to Hebrews 10:35–36, there is a great reward coming after you have done God's will. Keep moving and striving patiently for the manifestation of His will for your life. Also, it is important to remain focused, which will give you strength in your most difficult moments because you know that where you are going is greater than what you may be experiencing. Maintain a strong self-image, and you will survive.

Different Doesn't Mean Inferior

But God gives to it the body that He plans and sees
fit, and to each kind of seed a body of its own.
—1 Corinthians 15:38 (AMPC)

You are inferior to no one. God uniquely designed you. When you compare yourself to others, you will notice some obvious contrasts. It doesn't make them better than you; it just makes them different. That's OK because that was the Creator's intent. You must understand and appreciate your God-given differences; otherwise, there will always be inner conflicts.

Your outward conflicts are a result of what is happening inwardly. I am sure you will agree that a majority of your inner struggles exist because you feel as if you do not quite measure up when compared to others. You spend countless hours trying to be someone you are not because you believe that who you are is not good enough. When God created you, He created a marvelous work.

I will praise thee; for I am fearfully and wonderfully made: marvellous are thy works; and that my soul knoweth right well. My substance was not hid from thee, when I was made in secret, and curiously wrought in the lowest parts of the earth. Thine eyes did see my substance, yet being unperfect; and in thy book all my members were written, which in continuance were fashioned, when as yet there was none of them. (Psalm 139:14–16 KJV)

Do not turn away from everything that is in you, thinking it will help you and that others will be comfortable and accepting of who you are. God designed you as He saw fit. You are not like anyone you know. You are just like God wanted you to be—different.

What makes you different? Is it your sense of style; is it your humor; is it your drive; or is it the clothes you wear? No, being you is being different. You do not have to wear exotic hairstyles or sport exotic clothes or expensive cars to be different. Every time you grace a room with your presence, there is not one person there who is like you. You are an original. Even if they are sporting the same outfit, inwardly you've got it going on. Remember that you are a beautiful work of art, and you are valuable to God and this world—so be you!

Celebrating ME

When was the last time you praised yourself? When was the last time you celebrated yourself for your accomplishments and abilities?

Write three things you appreciate about yourself.

_____

_____

_____

_____

Write three things you have accomplished. (It doesn't have to be major. Learn to celebrate the small and insignificant things you do.)

_____

_____

_____

_____

List any gifts, talents, or acquired skills you have mastered.

_____

_____

_____

_____

Celebrate ME Day

Set a day aside just for you. Celebrate yourself by shopping, sending yourself flowers, setting up a personal photo shoot, taking yourself to the movies and out to dinner, or buying yourself an "I appreciate me" gift. Go ahead. Others will learn how to bless you when they see you being good to yourself.

Discover You

But ye are a chosen generation, a royal priesthood, an holy nation,
a peculiar people; that ye should shew forth the praises of Him
Who hath called you out of darkness into His marvellous light.
—1 Peter 2:9 (KJV)

Who are you? Why were you created? You must understand the inherent
qualities that distinguish you from others around you—and then figure
out how to use those qualities to maximize all of your life's possibilities.
Your life is filled with promise! There is so much potential within you that
you have not begun to discover. It is time to take the journey. This will
be one of the most challenging yet rewarding expeditions that you will
undertake, but you must discover who you are. You can no longer continue
to be bait for the enemy.

Discovering yourself will not be an easy task when you lack self-
acceptance. Some of your past experiences have devalued your self-worth;
therefore, you have never felt worthy of having the attention of others—let
alone your own. Those past experiences and the people who have judged
you by them are wrong. You are not stupid. You are not weak. You are not
a failure. You are not incompetent, ugly, mean, selfish, too fat, too dark,
too skinny, too white, or any other derogatory term used to identify you
and connect you to past occurrences in life.

To discover yourself, you will have to stop looking for you in the eyes of
others and look to your Creator to see what He sees in you. In Ephesians,
Paul declares that you are "God's own handiwork ... recreated in Christ
Jesus" (Ephesians 2:10 AMPC). He took His hands and fashioned you
according to His purpose and His design.

God gave you purpose—and then He designed you according to that
purpose. Next, He supplied you with all you will ever need to fulfill that
purpose. Dr. Myles Munroe's *In Pursuit of Purpose* said, "The purpose of
something determines its design. The design determines needs." Wow!
The latter part of Ephesians 2:10 assures you that God created you so you
could do the good works that He predestined for you. He wants you to

take the paths He prepared and live "the good life which He prearranged and made ready" (Ephesians 2:10 AMPC) for you to live. Don't compare your needs to the needs of others because you don't share the same design. Being jealous is a waste of time since God will only do for you what He has placed within you. God has already placed everything you need along the path that He has created. He is just waiting on you to rediscover what He has known all along.

Discovering yourself is not an overnight, one-time event. It is a journey. It will take you pulling back the layers that have developed over the years, and that have covered your inherent qualities. You will need to spend some quality time getting to know yourself, which requires self-reflecting. Self-reflecting is exploring and examining yourself: your perspectives, your thoughts, your attitudes, your experiences, and your actions.

Self-reflection will take you to the backstage of your life where you will uncover the sources of your behaviors. You should practice self-reflection often and incorporate the exercise of it into your life's journey. Through this process, you gain a better understanding of your emotions, strengths, and weaknesses, and as you self-reflect, you will experience a fresh new perspective that will lead you to self-assessment.

Taking a personal assessment is the gateway to self-discovery. You will assess where you are and compare it to where you are going. Socrates, a Greek philosopher, believed that a life that is never assessed is not worth living. Self-assessments keep you focused on what's important in your life and keep your thoughts clear and objective about your life. You will find what motivates you, and you will acquire insight into your innermost being. You will see how to move forward, and you will be inspired to dream and develop a renewed vision for your life.

Use the questions on the pages that follow as a guide to your journey of discovering you. This guide will assist you, but feel free to create your own questions that best fit your situation. After you answer the questions, take the time to write the vision for your life. If you already have one, then rewrite it from the newfound perspective you may discover for your life. There are some blank pages included for you to journal your thoughts as you work through this process.

Before you begin, there are three simple rules you should follow:

- Answer the questions honestly.
- Don't rush it. You may have to dig deep—so be patient with the process.
- Find support. You may have to partner with someone you trust and talk through some of the layers that are a bit painful.

Warning: Be sure to choose someone who is connected to the Spirit of the Lord and who has gone on a journey of self-discovery. Also, choose someone who won't just agree with you and who will encourage you to push through the hard places.

Discover You

What makes you different? List those inherent qualities of character that distinguish you from people around you.

_____

_____

_____

List at least three strengths and three weaknesses of character.

Strengths

_____

_____

_____

Weaknesses

_____

_____

_____

How can you improve your areas of weakness?

_____

_____

_____

What matters most to you?

_____

_____

_____

What motivates you?

_____Helping people

_____Solving problems

_____Accomplishing a goal

_____Receiving a reward

_____Being needed

_____Learning new things

_____Recognition and appreciation

_____Power and fame

_____Creating something new

_____Working with a team

_____Coaching and mentoring

_____Other (_____)

What activities do you enjoy doing?

_____

_____

_____

Other Assessments: What have you failed in the past? How did you respond?

_____

_____

_____

Reflection: What could you have done differently?

_____

_____

_____

Without counsel purposes are disappointed: but in the
multitude of counsellors they are established.
—Proverbs 15:22 (KJV)

My Vision

The Word declares "where there is no vision, the people perish" (Proverbs 29:18 KJV). The word *perish* in the Hebrew language means "to cast off restraints" (Strong 2010). A vision will direct you toward God's purpose and design for your life. It will keep you from yielding to distractions, and you won't occupy time doing worthless activities. What do you see yourself doing in this life?

_____

_____

_____

_____

_____

_____

_____

_____

_____

_____

_____

_____

_____

_____

_____

Write the vision and make it plain upon tables.
—Habakkuk 2:2 (KJV)

My Thoughts

_____

_____

_____

_____

_____

_____

_____

_____

_____

_____

_____

_____

_____

_____

_____

_____

_____

_____

_____

_____

_____

In the multitude of my [anxious] thoughts within
me, Your comforts cheer and delight my soul!
—Psalm 94:19 (AMPC)

My Thoughts

_____

_____

_____

_____

_____

_____

_____

_____

_____

_____

_____

_____

_____

_____

_____

_____

_____

_____

_____

In the multitude of my [anxious] thoughts within
me, Your comforts cheer and delight my soul!
—Psalm 94:19 (AMPC)

My Thoughts

_____

_____

_____

_____

_____

_____

_____

_____

_____

_____

_____

_____

_____

_____

_____

_____

_____

_____

_____

_____

In the multitude of my [anxious] thoughts within
me, Your comforts cheer and delight my soul!
—Psalm 94:19 (AMPC)

My Thoughts

_____

_____

_____

_____

_____

_____

_____

_____

_____

_____

_____

_____

_____

_____

_____

_____

_____

_____

_____

In the multitude of my [anxious] thoughts within
me, Your comforts cheer and delight my soul!
—Psalm 94:19 (AMPC)

My Thoughts

_____

_____

_____

_____

_____

_____

_____

_____

_____

_____

_____

_____

_____

_____

_____

_____

_____

_____

_____

_____

In the multitude of my [anxious] thoughts within
me, Your comforts cheer and delight my soul!
—Psalm 94:19 (AMPC)

My Thoughts

_____

_____

_____

_____

_____

_____

_____

_____

_____

_____

_____

_____

_____

_____

_____

_____

_____

_____

_____

_____

In the multitude of my [anxious] thoughts within
me, Your comforts cheer and delight my soul!
—Psalm 94:19 (AMPC)

My Thoughts

In the multitude of my [anxious] thoughts within
me, Your comforts cheer and delight my soul!
—Psalm 94:19 (AMPC)

My Thoughts

_____

_____

_____

_____

_____

_____

_____

_____

_____

_____

_____

_____

_____

_____

_____

_____

_____

_____

_____

In the multitude of my [anxious] thoughts within
me, Your comforts cheer and delight my soul!
—Psalm 94:19 (AMPC)

My Thoughts

_____

_____

_____

_____

_____

_____

_____

_____

_____

_____

_____

_____

_____

_____

_____

_____

_____

_____

_____

In the multitude of my [anxious] thoughts within
me, Your comforts cheer and delight my soul!
—Psalm 94:19 (AMPC)

My Thoughts

_____

_____

_____

_____

_____

_____

_____

_____

_____

_____

_____

_____

_____

_____

_____

_____

_____

_____

In the multitude of my [anxious] thoughts within
me, Your comforts cheer and delight my soul!
—Psalm 94:19 (AMPC)

My Thoughts

_____

_____

_____

_____

_____

_____

_____

_____

_____

_____

_____

_____

_____

_____

_____

_____

_____

_____

_____

_____

_____

In the multitude of my [anxious] thoughts within
me, Your comforts cheer and delight my soul!
—Psalm 94:19 (AMPC)

My Thoughts

_____

_____

_____

_____

_____

_____

_____

_____

_____

_____

_____

_____

_____

_____

_____

_____

_____

_____

_____

In the multitude of my [anxious] thoughts within
me, Your comforts cheer and delight my soul!
—Psalm 94:19 (AMPC)

My Thoughts

_____

_____

_____

_____

_____

_____

_____

_____

_____

_____

_____

_____

_____

_____

_____

_____

_____

_____

_____

_____

_____

_____

In the multitude of my [anxious] thoughts within
me, Your comforts cheer and delight my soul!
—Psalm 94:19 (AMPC)

My Thoughts

_____

_____

_____

_____

_____

_____

_____

_____

_____

_____

_____

_____

_____

_____

_____

_____

_____

_____

_____

_____

In the multitude of my [anxious] thoughts within
me, Your comforts cheer and delight my soul!
—Psalm 94:19 (AMPC)

My Thoughts

In the multitude of my [anxious] thoughts within
me, Your comforts cheer and delight my soul!
—Psalm 94:19 (AMPC)

My Thoughts

_____

_____

_____

_____

_____

_____

_____

_____

_____

_____

_____

_____

_____

_____

_____

_____

_____

_____

_____

_____

In the multitude of my [anxious] thoughts within
me, Your comforts cheer and delight my soul!
—Psalm 94:19 (AMPC)

My Thoughts

_____

_____

_____

_____

_____

_____

_____

_____

_____

_____

_____

_____

_____

_____

_____

_____

_____

_____

_____

_____

In the multitude of my [anxious] thoughts within
me, Your comforts cheer and delight my soul!
—Psalm 94:19 (AMPC)

My Thoughts

_____

_____

_____

_____

_____

_____

_____

_____

_____

_____

_____

_____

_____

_____

_____

_____

_____

_____

_____

_____

In the multitude of my [anxious] thoughts within
me, Your comforts cheer and delight my soul!
—Psalm 94:19 (AMPC)

My Thoughts

In the multitude of my [anxious] thoughts within
me, Your comforts cheer and delight my soul!
—Psalm 94:19 (AMPC)

My Thoughts

_____

_____

_____

_____

_____

_____

_____

_____

_____

_____

_____

_____

_____

_____

_____

_____

_____

_____

_____

_____

_____

_____

_____

In the multitude of my [anxious] thoughts within
me, Your comforts cheer and delight my soul!
—Psalm 94:19 (AMPC)

My Thoughts

_____

_____

_____

_____

_____

_____

_____

_____

_____

_____

_____

_____

_____

_____

_____

_____

_____

_____

_____

_____

In the multitude of my [anxious] thoughts within
me, Your comforts cheer and delight my soul!
—Psalm 94:19 (AMPC)

My Thoughts

_____

_____

_____

_____

_____

_____

_____

_____

_____

_____

_____

_____

_____

_____

_____

_____

_____

_____

_____

_____

_____

In the multitude of my [anxious] thoughts within
me, Your comforts cheer and delight my soul!
—Psalm 94:19 (AMPC)

My Thoughts

_____

_____

_____

_____

_____

_____

_____

_____

_____

_____

_____

_____

_____

_____

_____

_____

_____

_____

_____

_____

_____

In the multitude of my [anxious] thoughts within
me, Your comforts cheer and delight my soul!
—Psalm 94:19 (AMPC)

My Thoughts

_____

_____

_____

_____

_____

_____

_____

_____

_____

_____

_____

_____

_____

_____

_____

_____

_____

_____

_____

_____

_____

In the multitude of my [anxious] thoughts within
me, Your comforts cheer and delight my soul!
—Psalm 94:19 (AMPC)

It's All in a Name

A good name is rather to be chosen than great riches,
and loving favour rather than silver and gold.
—Proverbs 22:1 (KJV)

According to scripture, a name is very important. Names are used to describe character and show personality. What is your name? What do you call yourself? What do people call you? People have been naming you all your life. It began with your parents giving you your name at birth, and then you may have also been labeled and named by others. People will label and name you based on their judgments of you. If you are not careful, you will buy into their judgments and answer to the name they give you. It's all in a name.

Be careful about being named by others, because people name or label items in order to control and show possession.

> God said, "Let us make man in our image, after our likeness: and let them have dominion over the fish of the sea, and over the fowl of the air, and over the cattle, and over all the earth, and over every creeping thing that creepeth upon the earth." (Genesis 1:26 KJV)

God purposed that man would have dominion over the fish, fowl, cattle, and over all the earth. Now watch this:

> And out of the ground the Lord God formed every beast of the field, and every fowl of the air; and brought them unto Adam to see what he would call them: and whatsoever Adam called every living creature, that was the name thereof. And Adam gave names to all cattle, and to the foul of the air, and to every beast of the field. (Genesis 2:19–20 KJV)

God purposed and designed man to dominate creation. He had to allow man to name every living creature. Anything you name, you control. Anything you control, you have the right to name. Do not allow others to declare who you are. If you allow others to proclaim who you are, you are giving them permission to dominate you—and you become subject to them.

According to Myles Munroe, "When you allow others to declare who you are, you are submitting your rights to them, and you must be prepared for the consequences." Creation is subject to humankind. Man disobeyed God, not creation, but creation is feeling the effects.

In Romans 8:19–22, Paul declares that creation is exposed to decay and corruption, not because of some fault on its part. Creation is feeling the consequences. Paul points out that creation is groaning and travailing in pain, waiting for the manifestation of the sons of God so that it can be delivered from the bondage of corruption. If people name you, they control you—and you will bear the consequences.

Another reason you should be careful about being named by others is that you become what you hear. If the name or label does not agree with God's Word and His plan for your life, do not adhere to it. Words are powerful. Jesus said, "The words that I speak unto you, they are spirit, and they are life" (John 6:63 KJV).

Allowing others to name you can create the wrong self-image within you. If they call you by the wrong name, you will spend your life trying to be something you are not:

> And God said, Let Us make man in Our image, after Our likeness: and let them have dominion over the fish of the sea, and over the fowl of the air, and over the cattle, and over all the earth, and over every creeping thing that creepeth upon the earth. (Genesis 1:26 KJV)

In this verse, the Hebrew word for *man* is Adam, which means "mankind or human being" (Strong 2010). This meaning suggests both male and female. In verses 27-28, it goes on to say that He created them in His image as male and female. Then He blessed them, and He spoke to them to be fruitful, and multiply, and replenish the earth.

God had a plan in mind for creating a nation of believers. He designed humankind (male and female) to accomplish His purpose, and He supplied them with everything they needed (the garden of Eden) to fulfill this call. What happened? In Genesis 2:21–23, God took a rib from Adam, made a woman, and brought her to the man. When the man first laid eyes upon her, he said, "This is now bone of my bones, and flesh of my flesh: she shall be called Woman, because she was taken out of Man" (Genesis 2:23 KJV). He saw her and called her based on what she was created from and not based on what she was created for: her purpose. She knew God before she knew him. Man's mistake was that he saw her in relation to himself and not in relation to God.

People see you and call you based on where you come from, who your parents are, the color of your skin, the size of the clothes you wear, your educational background, the car you drive, or the size of your residence. People are not God, and unless God reveals His plan to them, they can only call you based upon what they see of you through your personal appearance or actions. He said that He was creating them male and female in His image and after His likeness. His commands to them were to be fruitful, to multiply, and to replenish the earth. God did not create her for man but for Himself:

> Unto the woman He said, I will greatly multiply thy sorrow and thy conception; in sorrow thou shalt bring forth children; and thy desire shall be to thy husband, and he shall rule over thee. (Genesis 3:16 KJV)

Here, God reveals the woman's purpose. She will conceive and bring forth children. Her desire will be for her husband, and he will rule over her. Now, let's look at Adam's response:

> And Adam called his wife's name Eve; because she was the mother of all living. (Genesis 3:20 KJV)

In verse 20, Adam called his wife's name Eve, which in the Hebrew language means the "mother of all living" (Strong 2010). Hearing God's conversation with the woman, Adam realized her purpose and gave her the name Eve. The name Eve agrees with what God designed and declared. It is all in a name. She was more than just bone of his bone and flesh of his flesh. When Adam called her Woman, it was misleading because that name did not call forth her purpose. Not knowing her identity, Eve yielded to a different voice (the serpent). Eve was searching for significance when her life already had meaning because God created her to participate in the nurturing of creation, which was to be fruitful and multiply.

Productivity is possible where purpose is known and declared. Adam and Eve heard God say that she was the mother of all living. Then Adam began to call her by the name that represented what she was called to be, which was Eve. I believe that everything in Eve began to line up and function to cause her purpose to be fulfilled because it was after the declaration of that revelation that she bore children.

What you and others call you is very important. Another witness to this truth is Abraham. God changed Abram's name to Abraham, which meant the "father of a multitude" (Strong 2010). Every time anyone would call out his name, they were saying "father of a multitude," calling forth Abraham's "being." Although he was beyond his years of reproduction, the calling of that name brought life to his body. You can have the same result. The name you answer to can either ignite or destroy your purpose. Words have power. His will for your life can manifest when the name you are called agrees with what God says about you. What should your name be? What are people calling you? Is it in agreement with what God has purposed for you? Will it ignite your being and cause you to live a purposeful and fruitful life?

It's in a Name

Your Name:

_____

What does your name mean?

_____

List three words that describe you.

_____

_____

Give three names people call you.

_____

_____

Does your description match what people call you?

_____

If you could change your name, what would it be?

_____

What does that name mean?

_____

_____

A good name is rather to be chosen than great riches.
—Proverbs 22:1 (KJV)

Finding ME

For the earnest expectation of the creature waiteth
for the manifestation of the sons of God.
—Romans 8:19 (KJV)

Are you lost? Are you sure you are in the right place and doing the right
thing? Wherever you are, it is not too far that you and God cannot get it
back on track:

> In the beginning God created the heaven and the earth.
> And the earth was without form, and void; and darkness
> was upon the face of the deep. And the Spirit of God
> moved upon the face of the waters. (Genesis 1:1–2 KJV)

> Every good gift and every perfect gift is from above"
> (James 1:17 KJV)

If everything God creates is good, why was the earth without form,
void, and dark? Something happened to cause the earth to be void.
Theologians believe that when Lucifer was thrown out of heaven, he and
his angels came to earth and destroyed God's creation.

When God created you, you were good. You were not created confused,
broken, depressed, sick, or hurting. But something happened in time,
which caused your life to be dark and void. Notice, there is no mention of
the cause for the darkness in that scripture. Why? The Holy Spirit revealed
to me that the cause was not as important as the answer, and the answer
was in the verse that followed:

> And God said, "Let there be light: and there was light."
> (Genesis 1:3 KJV)

God saw beyond the darkness and spoke to what He knew He had
created. To find yourself, you must look beyond the brokenness and
confusion that the pain in life has caused and speak to the good you

were created to be. At this point, don't let the cause of the confusion or brokenness be your focus. According to Romans 8:28, all things operate mutually for the good.

You have an opportunity to see the purpose of the pain and allow it to bring forth a better you. For example, Jesus learned obedience through the agonizing things that He experienced. Although it was painful, it earned Him a name that today is above all names. It also gave Him a seat in heavenly places "far above all principality, and power, and might, and dominion, and every name that is named" (Ephesians 1:21 KJV).

Brokenness is not meant to destroy you or cause you to be lost. You became lost while trying to cope with the pain that life's challenges brought. You changed direction because you were trying to escape the pain, avoid the problems, and please the people. Now, it is time to find yourself and get your life on track. Getting your life on track will require regaining your perspective on life, your passion for life, your position in life, and your profession about life.

Regain Your Perspective on Life

You must view everything in their true relation and relative importance. What is important to you? What matters most? Is it the car you drive, the house you live in, the friends you have, your family, or your job—or is it God? Take the time to prioritize your life. You can rid your life of the chaos and frustration through order. Order is achieved through taking an objective look at your life and then arranging what you see into a manageable form. Start by deciding what is important and then prune away the things you have added over the years that do not contribute to productivity.

Put God first. God has a plan, purpose, and design for your life. All that you have and all that you are began with Him. In Acts 17:27–28, Paul declares to the men of Athens that they should seek the Lord in hopes that they might find Him because it is in Him that "we live, and move, and have our being" (Acts 17:28 KJV).

You cannot do it without Him. No one knows creation like the Creator, and only He can direct your way:

> I know that [the determination of] the way of a man is
> not in himself; it is not in man [even in a strong man or
> in a man at his best] to direct his [own] steps. (Jeremiah
> 10:23 AMPC)

Even at your best, you will mess it up. You must put His desire for your life first and make His will a priority. Put God first on your to-do list.

The next step is getting yourself together! Spend time focusing on yourself. This may be difficult if you were taught to put God first, others second, and yourself last. It starts with God, it extends to you, and then it embraces others.

Your aim is to live your life in service to others, but you cannot give to others what you do not possess. It is a challenge to minister healing when you need healing and minister peace when you have not learned how to deal with the confusion in your own life. Do not escape your pain by living your life through others. Deal with your pain, get healed, and smile again.

Stop making excuses because everyone has challenges. Some people face challenges, and some people hide. Stop hiding and start healing. Face life and deal with it. God has a way of escape for you. The situation you are in may be difficult, but there is an answer in the Word of God that will lead to victory and wholeness. Spend time encouraging and ministering to yourself. You are the master of your destiny. You hold the keys to your success. You must work on your inner struggles in order to have strength to conquer the chaos that everyday challenges can bring into your world.

Next, live your life being a benefit to others.

> Look not every man on his own things, but every man
> also on the things of others. (Philippians 2:4 KJV)

After the power of God transforms your life, He wants to change the lives of others. He will accomplish that through you because now you can open your healed heart and allow the love of God to operate through you to help heal the hearts of others. Somebody needs your assistance. Just as God sent someone to get you started on your journey toward purpose, He wants you to be that spark in the life of others. Allow God to serve humanity through you so others can experience the joy of living life with purpose. Earnestly work on you, rise up, and then be a support for others.

Regain Your Passion for Life

Find the joy in being you. Have you lost your zeal for life? Has life become mundane? If you answered yes to either of those questions, you are saying that you have lost your passion. Passion is a strong desire toward your purpose that will drive you to see your life's assignment fulfilled. Regain your passion by dreaming and desiring again:

> Hope deferred makes the heart sick, but when the desire is fulfilled, it is a tree of life. (Proverbs 13:12 AMPC)

You have delayed your dreams long enough. You have limited your life's possibilities long enough! The best way to overcome the failures of your past is to create your future. Take off the limitations and dream. You lose heart when you limit yourself by what you have. Listen. Do not let what you cannot do stop you from doing what you can.

It does not cost you anything to dream, so use your imagination to dream beyond your means. He "is able to carry out His purpose and do superabundantly ... infinitely beyond our highest prayers, desires, thoughts, hopes, or dreams" (Ephesians 3:20 AMPC). Let your imagination take you there, and God will get you there.

The late Pastor Darryl Daniels said, "Start where you are. Use what you have, and do all you can do." Then watch God. Go after your success with fervor and enthusiasm. Who told you that you could not do and be whatever you desire? Whether it is owning your own business, starting a ministry, writing a book, writing a song, or traveling, you can do it. Stop putting off your success. Don't be afraid to dream!

Regain Your Position in Life

You were meant to be a success story that others would aspire to be like. You are better than where you are, but you must understand and live in God's purpose for your life. The Word says that you are the head and not the tail. It tells you that you are above only and not beneath—and that you are more than a conqueror. Get back in position. What is your position?

In Luke 19, Jesus shares a parable about a nobleman who went into a far country and started a kingdom. He returned and called ten of his servants. He gave them ten pounds and said, "Occupy until I come."

The nobleman established a kingdom, hired servants, and gave them positions and the funds required to operate. Next, he commissioned them to work until he returned. God is expecting the same of you. He is establishing His kingdom here on earth. He created and ordained you in your mother's womb. He has made everything that you will need available to you, and He is expecting you to occupy (do the work) until His Son returns. You can regain your position in life by choosing to live for Him and not for others.

Find your occupation. Remember, you were purposed to an occupation in life that would bring glory to the Father. God created you—and then He placed you. The gifts and talents He gave you are to be used in the space He designed for you to occupy. You may have gotten off track and started living your life for applause and acceptance, but God has not changed His mind. Living for others will lead to an empty and unfulfilled life. Get out of there! Remember that life's fulfillment is in doing what you were created to do. Get in your position, explore all of your life's possibilities, and live.

Regain Your Profession about Life

Use your words to begin the change in your life. Remember how the earth was without form and void and darkness was upon the face of the deep? God did not create it that way. How do you think God felt when He saw something that was beautiful destroyed by the devil? Regardless of how He may have felt about the earth's condition, He was not moved by the darkness He saw. He knew He had purpose in mind when He created heaven and earth. He was not willing to let anything hinder that purpose. Not even the mistake of others could stop His plan. He feels the same way about your life.

How do you think He feels about your life being dark and void? He is not focused on the current condition of your life. He has not counted the mistakes you have made against you:

For the gifts and calling of God are without repentance. (Romans 11:29 KJV)

God will not change His mind and revoke His purpose for your life or withdraw the gifts and talents that He has given you. He is not willing to allow anyone or anything to hinder you.

You might say, "If my mistakes are not the problem, then what are?"

It is your deficient knowledge of the Word, poor understanding of God's love for you, and lack of desire and passion for life. He is waiting on you to get as passionate about your life's purpose as He is. When you find your passion for your life, what should you do? What did God do? He began the restoration process. What did God use to restore order on the earth?

> And the earth was without form, and void; and darkness was upon the face of the deep. And the Spirit of God moved upon the face of the waters. And God said, Let there be light: and there was light. (Genesis 1:2–3 KJV)

He used His Words. He saw darkness, but He did not speak darkness. Do not give place to the devil. Use words of faith to create your world and restore order to your life. Do not speak what you see.

The Lord has given you two sources. One source is God's written Word. Speak what the Word says about you. The Lord promises that His Word "shall not return … (without producing any effect), but it shall accomplish that which I please and purpose" (Isaiah 55:11 AMPC).

Build yourself by using God's Words to change how you feel and how you see yourself. Tell yourself that you are blessed and highly favored. Tell yourself that you can do all things through Christ that strengthens and sustains you. Tell yourself that you are the head and not the tail. Tell yourself that you are taking up your bed and walking into your new way of living.

The other source is God's rhema Word, which is based on His written Word. Rhema Word occurs when revelation of God's written Word is spoken to guide you in your current situation. It is the Holy Spirit revealing to you what God has planned specifically for you:

Howbeit when He, the Spirit of truth, is come, He will guide you into all truth: for He shall not speak of Himself; but whatsoever He shall hear, that shall He speak: and He will shew you things to come. (John 16:13 KJV)

Allow His Holy Spirit to move in your life, show you things to come, and bring all things to your remembrance. Give the Holy Spirit permission to lead and guide you—and give Him the opportunity to make intercession for you according to God's will. Whatever He speaks, that is what you speak and use to declare war on the enemy:

This charge I commit unto thee, son Timothy, according to the prophecies which went before on thee, that thou by them mightest war a good warfare. (1 Timothy 1:18 KJV)

You will have to fight to rise up and begin your journey toward purpose. Your greatest fight will be with yourself—your mind, your will, and your emotions—which have been subjected to years of fear, frustration, and doubt. You can overcome!

They overcame him by the blood of the Lamb and by the Word of their testimony. (Revelations 12:11 KJV)

Get passionate about your life, get the Word, and gain knowledge of who God is—and who you are in Him. Then keep confessing His Word until you gain the strength to arise and produce amazing results in your life!

The Called to Be ME Journal

How to Keep Your Called to Be ME Journal

Are you ready to begin your journey of self-discovery? Each day, you can plan your escape by making productive steps toward change. God promised to "carry out His purpose and do superabundantly … infinitely beyond your highest prayers, desires, thoughts, hopes, and dreams" (Ephesians 3:20 AMPC).

The Creator has a purpose for your life. Your life's fulfillment is in being what you were created to be. Find purpose—and you will find you. It is time for you to redirect, refocus, and recenter your life around the Creator's purpose and plan. This part of the journal is designed to help you:

- vocalize and visualize who you are and what you desire
- help you bring balance and wholeness to your life through prioritizing and giving yourself assignments

You will have to be intentional about assigning yourself tasks to complete. Each day, spend time in prayer and meditation over the Word concerning your life. This will be your greatest challenge, but you must start somewhere.

Some days, those steps will be big, and then some days, they will be small, but you must keep moving:

> The steps of a good man are ordered by the Lord. (Psalm 37:23 KJV)

Your life's journey has already been designed for you, and the Lord will direct you if you acknowledge Him. Before you begin your journal, here are some instructions to assist in the completing of each section:

> Daily Prayer: This is a prayer of submission and self-focus.

> Never Again: Use these pages to write down and vocalize the emotions, attitudes, viewpoints, and character traits that you desire to change.

I Am Confession: You change what you see when you change what you say. This confession is based on scripture. It will help you create a new image of who you are.

I Am: "As he thinketh in his heart, so is He" (Proverbs 23:7 KJV). Paste words of affirmation and faith on this page that describes who you are.

My Priorities: Setting priorities helps bring balance to your life. To live a life free of frustration, you must prioritize and put in order those things that you value.

My Assignment: Write what you want to accomplish, what you need to accomplish it, and who you need to contact to assist you. Then write your progress or setbacks.

My Desires: Make a list of the places you would go, purchases you would make, and things you would accomplish if there were no limitations. Then use the pages that follow to paste photos or pictures to create a visual for your faith.

My Petition: The Word promises that if you ask anything according to His will, He hears you. This page will help you develop your prayer life by showing you how to take the promises of God and pray them over your requests. Write out your petitions and find a promise in the Word that you can pray. Then rewrite that promise to develop your daily confession, which will shape your belief system.

My Recovery Confession: This is a good confession to speak over your life.

My New Look: Now that you have embraced who you are and discovered your purpose, use these pages to chronicle your journey forward. Let's erase your past by creating your future!

Daily Prayer

Lord, strengthen me in my inner man by Your Spirit. Thank You for giving me a discerning spirit to direct me as it relates to the spiritual, emotional, and personal needs of others—and give me the courage to look within myself and face my own deficiencies of character and development.

Lord, give me a hunger and thirst for Your Word so that Your Word may bring knowledge and wisdom to empower my life for living. By faith and according to Your Word, I open my eyes to see, my ears to hear, and my heart to receive the light of Your Truth, and I embrace all the possibilities Your Truth was sent to bring to me.

Never Again

Never again will I

_____

_____

Because

_____

_____

Never again will I

_____

_____

Because

_____

_____

Never again will I

_____

_____

Because

_____

_____

Therefore if any man be in Christ, he is a new creature: old
things are passed away; behold, all things are become new.
—2 Corinthians 5:17 (KJV)

Never Again

Never again will I

_____

_____

Because

_____

_____

Never again will I

_____

_____

Because

_____

_____

Never again will I

_____

_____

Because

_____

_____

Therefore if any man be in Christ, he is a new creature: old
things are passed away; behold, all things are become new.
—2 Corinthians 5:17 (KJV)

Never Again

Never again will I

_____

_____

Because

_____

_____

Never again will I

_____

_____

Because

_____

_____

Never again will I

_____

_____

Because

_____

_____

Therefore if any man be in Christ, he is a new creature: old
things are passed away; behold, all things are become new.
—2 Corinthians 5:17 (KJV)

Never Again

Never again will I

_____

_____

Because

_____

_____

Never again will I

_____

_____

Because

_____

_____

Never again will I

_____

_____

Because

_____

_____

Therefore if any man be in Christ, he is a new creature: old
things are passed away; behold, all things are become new.
—2 Corinthians 5:17 (KJV)

Never Again

Never again will I

_____

_____

Because

_____

_____

Never again will I

_____

_____

Because

_____

_____

Never again will I

_____

_____

Because

_____

_____

Therefore if any man be in Christ, he is a new creature: old
things are passed away; behold, all things are become new.
—2 Corinthians 5:17 (KJV)

Never Again

Never again will I

_____

_____

Because

_____

_____

Never again will I

_____

_____

Because

_____

_____

Never again will I

_____

_____

Because

_____

_____

Therefore if any man be in Christ, he is a new creature: old
things are passed away; behold, all things are become new.
—2 Corinthians 5:17 (KJV)

I Am Confession

He completes me! I am in Jesus Christ, and I have come to the fullness of life because He completes me, making me self-sufficient in His sufficiency. It is in Him that I live, move, and have my being.

I am strong, and I am able to overcome all things. His grace, favor, loving-kindness, and mercy empower me and enable me to bear any trouble.

There is nothing I cannot achieve for I am ready for anything and equal to all things through Jesus Christ who instills inner strength into me.

Nothing will overwhelm me or overtake me. He gives me strength for all things, and victory over any and all addictions, anger, arrogance, bitterness, depression, discouragement, disobedience, double-mindedness, disease, failure, fear, generational curses, grief, guilt, lack, pain, pride, poverty, rebellion, rejection, sadness, selfishness, sickness, shame, unforgiveness, and witchcraft.

In Him, I am forgiven. I am loved. I am saved. I am redeemed. I am justified. I am glorified. I am healed. I am delivered. I am free. I am restored. I am a new creature. I am mighty. I am chosen. I am called. I am predestined. I am established. I am covered. I am righteous. I am blessed. I am anointed. I am honored. I am favored. I am powerful. I am royalty. I am wise. I am prosperous. I am humble. I am victorious. I am an overcomer.

He completes me!

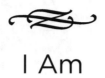

I Am

For as he thinketh in his heart, so is he.
—Proverbs 23:7 (KJV)

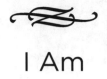

I Am

For as he thinketh in his heart, so is he.
—Proverbs 23:7 (KJV)

I Am

For as he thinketh in his heart, so is he.
—Proverbs 23:7 (KJV)

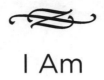

I Am

For as he thinketh in his heart, so is he.
—Proverbs 23:7 (KJV)

I Am

For as he thinketh in his heart, so is he.
—Proverbs 23:7 (KJV)

I Am

For as he thinketh in his heart, so is he.
—Proverbs 23:7 (KJV)

I Am

For as he thinketh in his heart, so is he.
—Proverbs 23:7 (KJV)

I Am

For as he thinketh in his heart, so is he.
—Proverbs 23:7 (KJV)

My Priorities

After taking a look at your current priorities, you may need to rewrite your priorities. If so, reprioritize them on this page.

What you value in life will determine how you live your life.
—Stacia Pierce

_____

_____

_____

_____

_____

_____

_____

_____

_____

_____

_____

_____

_____

But seek ye first the kingdom of God, and His righteousness;
and all these things shall be added unto you.
—Matthew 6:33 (KJV)

My Priorities

After taking a look at your current priorities, you may need to rewrite your priorities. If so, reprioritize them on this page.

What you value in life will determine how you live your life.
—Stacia Pierce

_____

_____

_____

_____

_____

_____

_____

_____

_____

_____

_____

_____

But seek ye first the kingdom of God, and His righteousness;
and all these things shall be added unto you.
—Matthew 6:33 (KJV)

My Assignment

Today is: _____

I want to accomplish:

_____

_____

_____

I need:

_____

_____

_____

I need to contact:

Name: _____

Number: _____

Name: _____

Number: _____

Comments:

_____

_____

I count not myself to have apprehended: but this one
thing I do, forgetting those things which are behind, and
reaching forth unto those things which are before.
—Philippians 3:13 (KJV)

My Assignment

Today is: _____

I want to accomplish:

_____

_____

_____

I need:

_____

_____

_____

I need to contact:

Name: _____

Number: _____

Name: _____

Number: _____

Comments:

_____

_____

I count not myself to have apprehended: but this one
thing I do, forgetting those things which are behind, and
reaching forth unto those things which are before.
—Philippians 3:13 (KJV)

My Assignment

Today is: _____

I want to accomplish:

_____

_____

_____

I need:

_____

_____

_____

I need to contact:

Name: _____

Number: _____

Name: _____

Number: _____

Comments:

_____

_____

I count not myself to have apprehended: but this one
thing I do, forgetting those things which are behind, and
reaching forth unto those things which are before.
—Philippians 3:13 (KJV)

My Assignment

Today is: _____

I want to accomplish:

_____

_____

_____

I need:

_____

_____

_____

I need to contact:

Name: _____

Number: _____

Name: _____

Number: _____

Comments:

_____

_____

I count not myself to have apprehended: but this one
thing I do, forgetting those things which are behind, and
reaching forth unto those things which are before.
—Philippians 3:13 (KJV)

My Assignment

Today is: _____

I want to accomplish:

_____

_____

_____

I need:

_____

_____

_____

I need to contact.

Name: _____

Number: _____

Name: _____

Number: _____

Comments:

_____

_____

I count not myself to have apprehended: but this one
thing I do, forgetting those things which are behind, and
reaching forth unto those things which are before.
—Philippians 3:13 (KJV)

My Assignment

Today is: _____

I want to accomplish:

_____

_____

_____

I need:

_____

_____

_____

I need to contact:

Name: _____

Number: _____

Name: _____

Number: _____

Comments:

_____

_____

I count not myself to have apprehended: but this one
thing I do, forgetting those things which are behind, and
reaching forth unto those things which are before.
—Philippians 3:13 (KJV)

My Assignment

Today is: _____

I want to accomplish:

_____

_____

_____

I need:

_____

_____

_____

I need to contact:

Name: _____

Number: _____

Name: _____

Number: _____

Comments:

_____

_____

I count not myself to have apprehended: but this one
thing I do, forgetting those things which are behind, and
reaching forth unto those things which are before.
—Philippians 3:13 (KJV)

My Desires

If there were no limitations:

What would you achieve?

_____

_____

_____

_____

_____

What would you acquire?

_____

_____

_____

_____

Where would you go?

_____

_____

_____

_____

Delight thyself also in the Lord: and He shall
give thee the desires of thine heart.
—Psalm 37:4 (KJV)

My Desires

Find photos or pictures to represent those things that you desire having or doing and paste them on this page.

Delight thyself also in the Lord: and He shall
give thee the desires of thine heart.
—Psalm 37:4 (KJV)

My Desires

Find photos or pictures to represent those things that you desire having or doing and paste them on this page.

Delight thyself also in the Lord: and He shall
give thee the desires of thine heart.
—Psalm 37:4 (KJV)

My Desires

Find photos or pictures to represent those things that you desire having or doing and paste them on this page.

Delight thyself also in the Lord: and He shall
give thee the desires of thine heart.
—Psalm 37:4 (KJV)

My Desires

Find photos or pictures to represent those things that you desire having or doing and paste them on this page.

Delight thyself also in the Lord: and He shall
give thee the desires of thine heart.
—Psalm 37:4 (KJV)

My Desires

Find photos or pictures to represent those things that you desire having or doing and paste them on this page.

Delight thyself also in the Lord: and He shall
give thee the desires of thine heart.
—Psalm 37:4 (KJV)

My Desires

Find photos or pictures to represent those things that you desire having or doing and paste them on this page.

Delight thyself also in the Lord: and He shall
give thee the desires of thine heart.
—Psalm 37:4 (KJV)

My Desires

Find photos or pictures to represent those things that you desire having or doing and paste them on this page.

Delight thyself also in the Lord: and He shall
give thee the desires of thine heart.
—Psalm 37:4 (KJV)

My Desires

Find photos or pictures to represent those things that you desire having or doing and paste them on this page.

Delight thyself also in the Lord: and He shall
give thee the desires of thine heart.
—Psalm 37:4 (KJV)

My Desires

Find photos or pictures to represent those things that you desire having or doing and paste them on this page.

Delight thyself also in the Lord: and He shall
give thee the desires of thine heart.
—Psalm 37:4 (KJV)

My Desires

Find photos or pictures to represent those things that you desire having or doing and paste them on this page.

Delight thyself also in the Lord: and He shall
give thee the desires of thine heart.
—Psalm 37:4 (KJV)

My Desires

Find photos or pictures to represent those things that you desire having or doing and paste them on this page.

Delight thyself also in the Lord: and He shall
give thee the desires of thine heart.
—Psalm 37:4 (KJV)

My Desires

Find photos or pictures to represent those things that you desire having or doing and paste them on this page.

Delight thyself also in the Lord: and He shall
give thee the desires of thine heart.
—Psalm 37:4 (KJV)

My Petition

Date: _____

The Appeal: Write your request.

_____

_____

_____

The Assurance: Write the scriptural reference.

_____

_____

_____

The Affirmation: Put the scripture in your own words.

_____

_____

_____

I Believe: Write what you believe about what you are praying. Remember, you don't get what you pray for—you get what you believe when you pray.

_____

_____

_____

And this is the confidence that we have in Him, that, if we ask any thing according to His will, He heareth us: And if we know that He hear us, whatsoever we ask, we know that we have the petitions that we desired of Him.
—1 John 5:14–15 (KJV)

My Petition

Date: _____

The Appeal: Write your request.

_____

_____

_____

The Assurance: Write the scriptural reference.

_____

_____

_____

The Affirmation: Put the scripture in your own words.

_____

_____

_____

I Believe: Write what you believe about what you are praying. Remember, you don't get what you pray for—you get what you believe when you pray.

_____

_____

_____

And this is the confidence that we have in Him, that, if we
ask any thing according to His will, He heareth us: And
if we know that He hear us, whatsoever we ask, we know
that we have the petitions that we desired of Him.
—1 John 5:14–15 (KJV)

My Petition

Date: _____

The Appeal: Write your request.

_____

_____

_____

The Assurance: Write the scriptural reference.

_____

_____

_____

The Affirmation: Put the scripture in your own words.

_____

_____

_____

I Believe: Write what you believe about what you are praying. Remember, you don't get what you pray for—you get what you believe when you pray.

_____

_____

_____

And this is the confidence that we have in Him, that, if we
ask any thing according to His will, He heareth us: And
if we know that He hear us, whatsoever we ask, we know
that we have the petitions that we desired of Him.
—1 John 5:14–15 (KJV)

My Petition

Date: _____

The Appeal: Write your request.

_____

_____

_____

The Assurance: Write the scriptural reference.

_____

_____

_____

The Affirmation: Put the scripture in your own words.

_____

_____

_____

I Believe: Write what you believe about what you are praying. Remember, you don't get what you pray for—you get what you believe when you pray.

_____

_____

_____

And this is the confidence that we have in Him, that, if we
ask any thing according to His will, He heareth us: And
if we know that He hear us, whatsoever we ask, we know
that we have the petitions that we desired of Him.
—1 John 5:14–15 (KJV)

My Petition

Date: _____

The Appeal: Write your request.

_____

_____

_____

The Assurance: Write the scriptural reference.

_____

_____

_____

The Affirmation: Put the scripture in your own words.

_____

_____

_____

I Believe: Write what you believe about what you are praying. Remember, you don't get what you pray for—you get what you believe when you pray.

_____

_____

_____

And this is the confidence that we have in Him, that, if we
ask any thing according to His will, He heareth us: And
if we know that He hear us, whatsoever we ask, we know
that we have the petitions that we desired of Him.
—1 John 5:14–15 (KJV)

My Petition

Date: _____

The Appeal: Write your request.

_____

_____

_____

The Assurance: Write the scriptural reference.

_____

_____

_____

The Affirmation: Put the scripture in your own words.

_____

_____

_____

I Believe: Write what you believe about what you are praying. Remember, you don't get what you pray for—you get what you believe when you pray.

_____

_____

_____

And this is the confidence that we have in Him, that, if we
ask any thing according to His will, He heareth us: And
if we know that He hear us, whatsoever we ask, we know
that we have the petitions that we desired of Him.
—1 John 5:14–15 (KJV)

My Petition

Date: _____

The Appeal: Write your request.

_____

_____

_____

The Assurance: Write the scriptural reference.

_____

_____

_____

The Affirmation: Put the scripture in your own words.

_____

_____

_____

I Believe: Write what you believe about what you are praying. Remember, you don't get what you pray for—you get what you believe when you pray.

_____

_____

_____

And this is the confidence that we have in Him, that, if we
ask any thing according to His will, He heareth us: And
if we know that He hear us, whatsoever we ask, we know
that we have the petitions that we desired of Him.
—1 John 5:14–15 (KJV)

My Recovery Confession: Deuteronomy 28:1–14

Because I diligently listen to the voice of the Lord my God observing and doing all His commandments which He commands me, today the Lord my God will set me on high above all nations of the earth.

On the condition that I continue to listen to and obey His voice, I will be empowered and made to prosper by and be overtaken by His blessed promises everywhere I go and in everything I do and acquire.

I am blessed in my body, which is His temple, and I live in divine health.

The Lord will demand, charge, and decree blessings upon my life, causing it to be productive and fruitful wherever I go. I have success in everything I endeavor on my job, in my business, in my church, and in my community. My diligence will yield an increase in finances unto me in my pocketbook, bank accounts, savings accounts, mutual funds, and retirement funds.

I am blessed in my home whether I choose to reside in the city or country. My family is blessed, and wherever we travel, the blessings of the Lord are upon us, giving us favor and bringing increase to all that we set out to accomplish on the earth.

The Lord is my help and my strength. He will cause any opposition to my success to come to naught, and He will repay my enemies, causing them to take flight.

Because I adhere to His Word and walk according to His plan and purpose for my life, the Lord will establish me as His child. I am called, anointed, and appointed by Him for His service. He will endow me with favor with all people of the earth, and I will gain their trust and respect.

Again, I decree that I will maintain my focus on the Lord, His Word, His will, and His work for my life. In return, the Lord will "make me the head," opening unto me His kingdom, giving me access to His abundant supply, sharing His wisdom and secrets, keeping me successful, wealthy, and healthy, increasing me, and enlarging my territory and circle of influence so that I can be a blessing unto many nations.

My New Look

_____

_____

_____

_____

_____

_____

_____

_____

_____

_____

_____

_____

_____

_____

_____

_____

_____

_____

_____

_____

We were buried therefore with Him by the baptism into death, so that just as Christ was raised from the dead by the glorious [power] of the Father, so we too might [habitually] live _and_ behave in newness of life
—Romans 6:4 (AMPC)

My New Look

_____

_____

_____

_____

_____

_____

_____

_____

_____

_____

_____

_____

_____

_____

_____

_____

_____

_____

We were buried therefore with Him by the baptism into death, so that just as Christ was raised from the dead by the glorious [power] of the Father, so we too might [habitually] live *and* behave in newness of life
—Romans 6:4 (AMPC)

My New Look

_____

_____

_____

_____

_____

_____

_____

_____

_____

_____

_____

_____

_____

_____

_____

_____

_____

_____

_____

We were buried therefore with Him by the baptism into death, so that
just as Christ was raised from the dead by the glorious [power] of the
Father, so we too might [habitually] live _and_ behave in newness of life
—Romans 6:4 (AMPC)

My New Look

_____

_____

_____

_____

_____

_____

_____

_____

_____

_____

_____

_____

_____

_____

_____

_____

_____

_____

We were buried therefore with Him by the baptism into death, so that
just as Christ was raised from the dead by the glorious [power] of the
Father, so we too might [habitually] live _and_ behave in newness of life
—Romans 6:4 (AMPC)

My New Look

_____

_____

_____

_____

_____

_____

_____

_____

_____

_____

_____

_____

_____

_____

_____

_____

_____

_____

We were buried therefore with Him by the baptism into death, so that just as Christ was raised from the dead by the glorious [power] of the Father, so we too might [habitually] live _and_ behave in newness of life
—Romans 6:4 (AMPC)

My New Look

_____

_____

_____

_____

_____

_____

_____

_____

_____

_____

_____

_____

_____

_____

_____

_____

_____

_____

_____

_____

We were buried therefore with Him by the baptism into death, so that just as Christ was raised from the dead by the glorious [power] of the Father, so we too might [habitually] live _and_ behave in newness of life
—Romans 6:4 (AMPC)

My New Look

_____

_____

_____

_____

_____

_____

_____

_____

_____

_____

_____

_____

_____

_____

_____

_____

_____

_____

_____

_____

We were buried therefore with Him by the baptism into death, so that just as Christ was raised from the dead by the glorious [power] of the Father, so we too might [habitually] live *and* behave in newness of life
—Romans 6:4 (AMPC)

My New Look

_____

_____

_____

_____

_____

_____

_____

_____

_____

_____

_____

_____

_____

_____

_____

_____

_____

_____

_____

We were buried therefore with Him by the baptism into death, so that just as Christ was raised from the dead by the glorious [power] of the Father, so we too might [habitually] live _and_ behave in newness of life
—Romans 6:4 (AMPC)

My New Look

We were buried therefore with Him by the baptism into death, so that just as Christ was raised from the dead by the glorious [power] of the Father, so we too might [habitually] live *and* behave in newness of life
—Romans 6:4 (AMPC)

My New Look

_____

_____

_____

_____

_____

_____

_____

_____

_____

_____

_____

_____

_____

_____

_____

_____

_____

_____

_____

_____

We were buried therefore with Him by the baptism into death, so that just as Christ was raised from the dead by the glorious [power] of the Father, so we too might [habitually] live _and_ behave in newness of life —Romans 6:4 (AMPC)

My New Look

_____

_____

_____

_____

_____

_____

_____

_____

_____

_____

_____

_____

_____

_____

_____

_____

_____

_____

We were buried therefore with Him by the baptism into death, so that just as Christ was raised from the dead by the glorious [power] of the Father, so we too might [habitually] live *and* behave in newness of life
—Romans 6:4 (AMPC)

My New Look

_____
_____
_____
_____
_____
_____
_____
_____
_____
_____
_____
_____
_____
_____
_____
_____
_____
_____
_____

We were buried therefore with Him by the baptism into death, so that
just as Christ was raised from the dead by the glorious [power] of the
Father, so we too might [habitually] live *and* behave in newness of life
—Romans 6:4 (AMPC)

My New Look

_____

_____

_____

_____

_____

_____

_____

_____

_____

_____

_____

_____

_____

_____

_____

_____

_____

_____

_____

_____

We were buried therefore with Him by the baptism into death, so that just as Christ was raised from the dead by the glorious [power] of the Father, so we too might [habitually] live _and_ behave in newness of life
—Romans 6:4 (AMPC)

My New Look

We were buried therefore with Him by the baptism into death, so that just as Christ was raised from the dead by the glorious [power] of the Father, so we too might [habitually] live *and* behave in newness of life
—Romans 6:4 (AMPC)

My New Look

_____

_____

_____

_____

_____

_____

_____

_____

_____

_____

_____

_____

_____

_____

_____

_____

_____

_____

_____

We were buried therefore with Him by the baptism into death, so that just as Christ was raised from the dead by the glorious [power] of the Father, so we too might [habitually] live *and* behave in newness of life
—Romans 6:4 (AMPC)

My New Look

_____

_____

_____

_____

_____

_____

_____

_____

_____

_____

_____

_____

_____

_____

_____

_____

_____

_____

_____

We were buried therefore with Him by the baptism into death, so that just as Christ was raised from the dead by the glorious [power] of the Father, so we too might [habitually] live _and_ behave in newness of life
—Romans 6:4 (AMPC)

My New Look

_____

_____

_____

_____

_____

_____

_____

_____

_____

_____

_____

_____

_____

_____

_____

_____

_____

_____

_____

We were buried therefore with Him by the baptism into death, so that just as Christ was raised from the dead by the glorious [power] of the Father, so we too might [habitually] live _and_ behave in newness of life
—Romans 6:4 (AMPC)

My New Look

_____

_____

_____

_____

_____

_____

_____

_____

_____

_____

_____

_____

_____

_____

_____

_____

_____

_____

_____

We were buried therefore with Him by the baptism into death, so that
just as Christ was raised from the dead by the glorious [power] of the
Father, so we too might [habitually] live _and_ behave in newness of life
—Romans 6:4 (AMPC)

My New Look

_____

_____

_____

_____

_____

_____

_____

_____

_____

_____

_____

_____

_____

_____

_____

_____

_____

_____

_____

_____

We were buried therefore with Him by the baptism into death, so that just as Christ was raised from the dead by the glorious [power] of the Father, so we too might [habitually] live *and* behave in newness of life
—Romans 6:4 (AMPC)

My New Look

_____

_____

_____

_____

_____

_____

_____

_____

_____

_____

_____

_____

_____

_____

_____

_____

_____

_____

_____

We were buried therefore with Him by the baptism into death, so that just as Christ was raised from the dead by the glorious [power] of the Father, so we too might [habitually] live *and* behave in newness of life
—Romans 6:4 (AMPC)

My New Look

We were buried therefore with Him by the baptism into death, so that just as Christ was raised from the dead by the glorious [power] of the Father, so we too might [habitually] live *and* behave in newness of life
—Romans 6:4 (AMPC)

My New Look

_____

_____

_____

_____

_____

_____

_____

_____

_____

_____

_____

_____

_____

_____

_____

_____

_____

_____

_____

_____

We were buried therefore with Him by the baptism into death, so that just as Christ was raised from the dead by the glorious [power] of the Father, so we too might [habitually] live _and_ behave in newness of life
—Romans 6:4 (AMPC)

My New Look

_____

_____

_____

_____

_____

_____

_____

_____

_____

_____

_____

_____

_____

_____

_____

_____

_____

_____

_____

_____

_____

We were buried therefore with Him by the baptism into death, so that
just as Christ was raised from the dead by the glorious [power] of the
Father, so we too might [habitually] live _and_ behave in newness of life
—Romans 6:4 (AMPC)

My New Look

_____

_____

_____

_____

_____

_____

_____

_____

_____

_____

_____

_____

_____

_____

_____

_____

_____

We were buried therefore with Him by the baptism into death, so that just as Christ was raised from the dead by the glorious [power] of the Father, so we too might [habitually] live *and* behave in newness of life
—Romans 6:4 (AMPC)

My New Look

We were buried therefore with Him by the baptism into death, so that just as Christ was raised from the dead by the glorious [power] of the Father, so we too might [habitually] live *and* behave in newness of life
—Romans 6:4 (AMPC)

My New Look

We were buried therefore with Him by the baptism into death, so that just as Christ was raised from the dead by the glorious [power] of the Father, so we too might [habitually] live *and* behave in newness of life
—Romans 6:4 (AMPC)

My New Look

_____

_____

_____

_____

_____

_____

_____

_____

_____

_____

_____

_____

_____

_____

_____

_____

_____

_____

_____

We were buried therefore with Him by the baptism into death, so that just as Christ was raised from the dead by the glorious [power] of the Father, so we too might [habitually] live *and* behave in newness of life
—Romans 6:4 (AMPC)

My New Look

_____

_____

_____

_____

_____

_____

_____

_____

_____

_____

_____

_____

_____

_____

_____

_____

_____

_____

_____

_____

We were buried therefore with Him by the baptism into death, so that
just as Christ was raised from the dead by the glorious [power] of the
Father, so we too might [habitually] live _and_ behave in newness of life
—Romans 6:4 (AMPC)

My New Look

_____

_____

_____

_____

_____

_____

_____

_____

_____

_____

_____

_____

_____

_____

_____

_____

_____

_____

We were buried therefore with Him by the baptism into death, so that just as Christ was raised from the dead by the glorious [power] of the Father, so we too might [habitually] live _and_ behave in newness of life
—Romans 6:4 (AMPC)

My New Look

_____

_____

_____

_____

_____

_____

_____

_____

_____

_____

_____

_____

_____

_____

_____

_____

We were buried therefore with Him by the baptism into death, so that just as Christ was raised from the dead by the glorious [power] of the Father, so we too might [habitually] live _and_ behave in newness of life
—Romans 6:4 (AMPC)

REFERENCES

Munroe, Myles. 1992. *In Pursuit of Purpose*. Shippensburg, PA: Destiny Image.

Strong, James. 2010. *Strong's Exhaustive Concordance of the Bible*. Nashville: Thomas Nelson Publishers.

Printed in the United States
by Baker & Taylor Publisher Services